CHAKRA BALANCING FOR PEOPLE

Restore Holistic Wellness, Stimulate Healing, and Create a Mindful Lifestyle in 7 Days or Less

By Marta Tuchowska

Copyright © 2015 by Marta Tuchowska

TABLE OF CONTENTS

Introduction

Chakras, Inner Energy, and Holistic Wellness

Have you ever wondered why some people are always happy, balanced, and move forward with their goals and lives? Have you ever wondered why some people are able to create the life they want and live their dream? Finally, have you ever wondered why some people manage to remain focused, balanced, and composed, even when facing difficult situations and challenges in their lives?

Do you want to achieve real, vibrant health and holistic wellness? If the answer is yes, I would like to welcome you to the Holistic Seekers Club. We are in the same boat. We are looking for wellness, happiness, and fulfillment. We want real health from the inside out. We know that it's not only about eating healthy and exercising... Even though healthy activities like balanced nutrition and fitness help us feel better and re-balance our inner energy as well as calm chaotic thoughts and emotions, this is only the tip of the iceberg. Are you ready to dig deep?

I venture to say you are totally ready, because you have decided to pick up this book and invest in yourself. Yes! You see, investigating your spirituality and your connection with the Universe, as well as other people around you and most importantly your own emotions leads to holistic wellness.

What is holistic wellness? It's simple. It's when you feel good from the inside out. It's not only about looking good or having a sexy, fit body. You also want to be healthy and beautiful from the inside. You want to radiate positive energy so that you can empower other people. If you feel connected to your own personal energy, you know your 'why' and you have a clean vision. This is something that most people lack because they focus too much on all the "how-to" of our busy, faced-paced world, or get too obsessed with financial and social success. I am not judging or anything, I have been there myself. This is a part of the journey for everyone. Sooner or later everyone becomes a seeker, which is fantastic. Sooner or later, everyone will realize that there must be something like an inner force that can either work for us or against us. If used properly, it can guide us.

What is spirituality, then? The way I see it, spirituality is the art of becoming a better person. A better person for yourself and for this world. You want to create and embrace a stronger version of yourself. Forget about perfection and all those mainstream commercials selling you the perfect image of success.

As Jim Rohn says:

Success is not to be pursued. It is to be attracted by the person you become.

Spirituality also revolves around the concept of self-love and getting to know yourself better. No judgment, no expectations. Just progress and a smile on your face. Even if you are having a bad day today, or something is going wrong in your life, I believe that the practices from this book will help you change your mindset about it and align you with your real self. There is no mumbo-jumbo in this book, it is designed as a short and sweet guide for modern people who want to take action to find happiness and fulfillment in their lives. I am like you, and we are all coming from the same place. I am not a spiritual guru, this is what I always say in all of my books. I prefer to provide simple tools that you can add to your spiritual development tool box.

Spirituality and personal development go hand in hand. I believe that mastering spirituality is definitely about helping other people. Of course, first of all, you must get committed to helping yourself.

Think about it...

Energy pervades the universe. We know common kinds of energy such as heat, electricity, or light. Everything is energy, and this includes consciousness. Although mainstream science has not fully understood our minds yet, there are those who theorize that consciousness is made of energy fields.

Your different aspects – your intelligence, emotions, etc., exist as forms of energy that vibrate at particular levels. These various energies mesh with one another through invisible centers in your body that are called chakras, meaning "wheels" in Sanskrit.

To make it really simple for you, in case this is the first time you are hearing about it, chakras are vortexes of consciousness and life energy. These are located at many points in your body. There are 7 main chakras along the spine. The state of these chakras reflects and affects the health of the person in various levels: physical, psychological, and spiritual. There are also many minor chakras, but that's a topic for another book.

Since everything is energy, everything is vibrating at a certain frequency that is in tune with an individual chakra. Thus, these chakras are associated with many things, such as colors, tones, foods, qualities, functions, etc.

The chakras manage and transform energy into something that a person can use in his or her life. They need to be open and free of blockages to allow the energy to flow smoothly.

Your chakras can be affected in either a positive or negative way. Your lifestyle and way of perceiving the world are crucial to your chakras functioning optimally. Some people just need a little push to stimulate healing and balance themselves, whereas some people, usually those who experience traumas and pain, negative thinking, and other destructive habits or circumstances, may need to put in some more work and even ask for professional help. However, the good news is that the healing is possible. This book focuses on self-healing. See it as a 7 day program. Each day you will focus on a different chakra, brainstorm to ask yourself questions, and answer them at your convenience.

The tip number 1 for a more balanced and happier lifestyle that I want to give you is to talk to yourself and ask yourself questions. Brainstorm. Commit yourself to self-coaching. If I did it, you can do it too. You already know that this is not an easy wellness book with recipes. Don't get me wrong, these are important for your overall health and I have personally authored a couple of those types of books. However in *this* book, I'm taking a "dig deep" holistic approach. Your mind, soul, and body are interconnected. When you feel good from the inside out, you also feel more motivated to take action to pursue your ambitions and goals. It's like driving a car that works perfectly well and has a GPS so that you can enjoy the journey knowing you will always reach your destination. Then there is also you, the driver. You know where you're going, but when needed, you may take a different route. You know what to do and you feel confident.

Forget about negative emotions, stress, anger, frustration, and doubts. I want to help you to turn negative into positive. Of course, there will be bad days sometimes. In our existence, we are also meant to experience certain levels of pain. Luckily, thanks to a mindful approach that helps you realize how your chakras work and what to do to balance them, you will feel mentally and emotionally stronger.

Since the chakras are made up of the energies of consciousness, they affect different aspects of our lives. This explains why a healthy solar plexus chakra gives us self-confidence, or a blocked throat chakra can make us fumble over what to say.

Clairvoyants can see these chakras, while those who work with subtle energy can sense them via touch or devices such as pendulums. Kirlian photography claims to capture the aura and energy centers as well. However, it's enough to just observe, feel, and understand your own chakras.

Again, you can train yourself to perceive chakras, but you do not need to see the chakras to know if they're imbalanced or not. You simply have to observe yourself objectively to know their state. It's as simple as that. The more you do it, the more connections you will see between physical and emotional imbalances.

Like I mentioned earlier, there are numerous energy centers in the body, but many chakra development teachers agree that there are 7 major ones. These are found in certain locations along a person's spine. Each one of these is meaningfully linked with the body parts and organs near it.

Effects of Imbalances

A chakra can become imbalanced when it is blocked, when too little energy is being directed towards it, or when too much is poured into it. A block can happen if you store negative energy in the chakra or if you repress energy that is associated with that chakra. A depleted chakra can occur if energy is being directed away from the chakral center, such as when you deny a particular need. A hyperactive chakra is the product of excessive attention or effort directed towards a desire or aspect of life. This is no good either, but we have all been there. Again, not judging!

Imbalances in the chakras can lead to illnesses, anxiety and even mental disturbances.

Luckily, balancing your chakras is a natural tool that can be achieved via many natural therapies, body work, and mind work. The benefits of chakra balancing practice are numerous:

- You exercise your psychic abilities
- You improve awareness
- It enables you to work with subtle energies
- It allows you to reflect deeply on important matters
- It stabilizes emotions
- It gives clarity of thought
- It increases vitality
- It helps you understand yourself and other people better
- It opens up plenty of opportunities for you to take care of yourself
- It brings solutions to problems that you may be stuck with
- It can give you the resources to know how to assist other people as well
- It brings balance to your life

Remember that balancing chakras is not only a meditative technique or a spiritual practice, it is also a very thorough self-help method. Actually, many chakra balancing tools are also utilized in self-help and personal development. To achieve the best results, you need to follow up the meditations with real-life applications. You need to commit to it, but without getting too obsessed about it (not judging again, I used to be really obsessed about chakras!). Although the visualizations may be enough to improve your energy and change your situation, you will speed up the process if you also take action, face your fears, and work on your weak points.

Unfortunately, the way healing is being sold these days is an image of a person relaxing in a spa with a few stones and some nice aromas. Don't get me wrong, relaxation is really important and I love the spa. I studied spa therapy as well. All I am saying is that from now on, you need to make a commitment to working on your body, mind, and spirit. You need to employ your mind and your soul. While many natural remedies, herbs, spas, and yoga are extremely helpful in balancing your chakras and they are also discussed in this book, don't forget about the power of your mind. Don't force it, it will come. Simply talk to yourself and always ask yourself WHY. Sometimes you may not get the answer straight away. Just have faith. Your subconscious will be working for you in the meantime. It's like when you forget a name. The more you try to recall it, the harder it gets to remember. Suddenly, you stop thinking about it and it comes back to your mind. It happens because you were asking yourself, "Hold on, what was that name?" You made some initial effort and you let your subconscious mind work for you.

The problem is that many people focus on sailing against the wind, not with the wind.

I have also been guilty of that, everyone has. It's normal for us to keep focusing on what we cannot change, instead of accepting certain circumstances and focusing on what we can change, which is ourselves and our energy.

Now let the journey begin!

Just for your information, this book is focused mostly on chakra balancing. If you are looking for more information about chakras themselves (also in a practical way), you may want to check out my other book called: *Exploring Chakras and Discovering Holistic Wellness*.

However, even if you don't, for whatever reason, the book you are holding in your beautiful hands right now is designed both for those who have never heard of chakras before, as well as for those that have been seasoned and need to refresh their knowledge and get inspiration to enhance their existing healing practices.

Like I mentioned earlier, you can either read this book in a week and work on a different chakra every day, or simply go through the entire chakra balancing program at once and then focus on whichever of your chakras needs the most attention. You might also take your time and spend more than 1 day on each chakra. Just listen to your body and do what is right for you. If, during reading this book, you happen to have any questions or doubts, please write them all down and e-mail me:

info@holisticwellnessproject.com

I will do my best to help you!

Now let the journey begin!

Relax, take a few deep breaths, burn an incense stick and listen to some meditation relaxation music if you want.

Thanks again for taking an interest in this guide,

Marta (Certified Massage Therapist, Reiki II Practitioner, Holistic Wellness Coach and a Lover of Life).

Disclaimer

The author of this book is not a doctor and it is not her intention to claim that the treatments described in this book can be a substitute for professional medical advice, standard medical treatments, therapy, or counseling. This book is for educational and informative purposes only, and it offers an overview of alternative therapies based on meditation and chakra balancing.

Natural and alternative therapies described in this book are not to be interpreted as a substitute for standard medical treatments. Before applying aromatherapy and other natural remedies, please consult with a naturopath or a medical doctor.

All information in this book has been carefully researched and checked for factual accuracy. However, the author and publishers make no warranty, expressed or implied, that the information contained herein is appropriate for every individual, situation or purpose, and assume no responsibility for errors or omission. The reader assumes the risk and full responsibility for all actions, and the author will not be held liable for any loss or damage, whether consequential, incidental, and special or otherwise that may result from the information presented in this publication. By purchasing this book you have agreed to the above-mentioned disclaimer.

Chapter 1 - Day 1 - The First Chakra - Get Your Power Back and Create Your Own Way

The first chakra is the root chakra, called Muladhara in Sanscrit (it literally means "root support"). Like a root, it connects us to the earth and nourishes us with life force. It regulates our survival instincts so that we will keep ourselves alive and present on this earth.

Because it is the first chakra, it serves as the foundation of all the others above it. It is said that without a healthy root chakra, it is very difficult to develop the other chakras. You can understand this better by considering Maslow's hierarchy of needs. According to this hierarchy, human needs can be classified into the following types:

1. Physical – air, water, food, sleep, health, etc.
2. Safety - protection from harsh conditions, crime, and instability
3. Love and belongingness – friendship, love, intimacy, and relationships of all kinds

4. Esteem – self-esteem, prestige, achievement
5. Cognitive – to understand things, to gain knowledge, to perceive meaning
6. Aesthetic – to enjoy beauty and pleasant things
7. Self-actualization – Fulfilling one's goals and potentials
8. Transcendence – Enabling others to attain self-actualization

Maslow's idea was that you must meet your needs on a certain rank before you could fulfill needs that are on a higher rank. As you can see, physical and safety needs are the first two items on the list, and they correspond to the root chakra.

In simpler words, you must take care of your basic needs before you can proceed to more complex activities that require your heart and attention. Keeping this survival instinct, the drive to keep yourself living in this world, is the work of the base chakra. It enkindles your strength to perform in different aspects of your life, so you must take care of it.

I always say that it's hard to pursue holistic wellness if you struggle to get through the month and pay your bills. It's also hard to achieve fulfillment and happiness if you focus too much on financial wellbeing and you become too obsessed about it, completely forgetting about other areas of your life. After all, we need money to live well. We should work to live, not the other way around. I have personally experienced both extreme scenarios - one when I was in debt because I had neglected the importance of finances and survival, and the other one when I became too obsessed about "making money" and lost an interest in life. Re-designing my life, leaving the city, living close to nature, and combining my personal interests and passion with my professional life gave me a balance that I needed. What was a real game changer for me was regular gratitude practice, something I truly recommend you do daily. You can either write it all down, say it in your mind, say it out loud, or even record it on your mobile and listen to it when you feel disconnected. Lack of gratitude can lead to many materialistic obsessions. I believe there is nothing wrong with accumulating wealth and abundance, as long as you make them work for you and your life. You don't want to be a prisoner of your materialistic expectations, right?

At the same time, you need to be strong enough to provide the best shelter for your body and mind. This includes basic needs, food, a roof, and safety for you and your loved ones. Neglecting those basic needs or expecting other people to take care of you is a sign of an underactive root chakra. A common judgment a label could be, "He or she is not responsible!" But we are not judging here. We are saying, exploring, accepting, and transforming!

To sum up:

An overactive root chakra provokes a person to place too much importance on his or her survival, as well as being prone to addictions to pursue pleasure in an unhealthy way, like with alcohol. One can also become addicted and dependent to sex, but in an unhealthy and abnormal way and disconnect from reality. The fight or flight response may become overwhelmingly powerful and result in an excess of anger or fear. On the other side of the spectrum, an underactive root chakra can produce instability and disassociation with reality. Addictions to substances or situations that provide a feeling of security may result.

Everyday Activities and Hobbies That Balance Your Root Chakra

-Cooking your favorite meals

-All kinds of crafts where you use your hands. Gardening is especially recommended because it helps you re-connect with nature

-Getting involved with charity

-Walking barefoot on the grass or beach

-Walking, swimming, or yoga

-Being out in nature and hugging trees (I know it sounds a bit hippie dippie, but it's a great dose of positive vibration- there we go again, another hippie dippie line!)

-Music- listen and dance to something with an energetic beat, something that you really enjoy

-Watch comedies and funny videos, laugh as much as you can. Personally, I love watching comedies with my loved ones.

Other Recommendations

-Choose more red foods (ex. tomatoes, apples, cherries, etc.) and food rich in protein (lean meat, organic eggs, quinoa, nuts)

- Eat foods like potatoes, carrots and turnips- foods that come from the ground

-Have a glass of wine a day. It's good for you. Relax and laugh. If you can, go out with people who are into different stuff than you are so that you get a chance to talk about everything you can and see different ways of living. Cultivate acceptance. Try to meet happy people who live the way they want, even if it's not your way of living.

-Start a gratitude journal. Really do it now. Or if you have one, go back to it now. Have a break from reading and do a few minutes of positive journaling.

-Transfer whatever amount of money you wish to charity, or give away some clothes and other items you don't need. This will also help you declutter your house, another activity that is crucial in getting grounded and balancing your first chakra.

Affirmations

- I trust my body
- I am healthy
- I am safe
- I belong to the world
- I love myself
- I love who I have become
- I feel balanced
- Even though I may take longer to achieve my goals, I accept myself
- I feel grateful that I am alive
- I am strong
- I feel safe and protected
- I let money work for me
- I provide security and love for my family
- I accept other people

- I respect other people and I let them respect me
- I let it go
- I am in control of my urges
- I am appreciated at work
- I am financially secure
- I am peaceful
- I accept reality and I accept others
- I am successful
- I am connected to nature
- Life is abundant

Aromatherapy

Strong scents like ylang-ylang, rose, cedar wood, bergamot, sandalwood, and other powerful earthy scents are excellent root chakra balancers. You can either burn them in a vaporizer or use a diffuser, or even do a self-massage treatment. For that, blend 5 drops of your chosen essential oil with a tablespoon of vegetable base oil such as coconut, argan, or sweet almond. It doesn't really matter as long as the oil is natural. Massage your sacral and lumbar zones. A word of caution for ylang-ylang, it's an aphrodisiac!

Incantations:

Lam (great to use in your meditations)

Crystals

As an additional natural therapy, you can pick up one or more of the following crystals: hematite, garnet, ruby bloodstone, or onyx. They will give you the extra feeling of protection and guidance. You can carry them with you in your bag or even as a piece of jewelry as you go about your day. You can also keep them on your nightstand or use them for meditation. Keep them in your hands, or use them to massage your lower back and sacral zone.

Yoga

Mudra: Position your arms straight with your hands resting on your knees. Touch the tips of your thumb and pointer fingers together (do this with each hand separately).

Yoga exercises for the root chakra involve the feet, legs, perineum, base of the spine, and the pelvic floor.

Sitting

Sit in a cross-legged position. Inhale, and upon exhaling, allow the bottom parts of your legs and pelvis to touch the ground.

Mountain Pose

Stand with bare feet. Breathe in and out with your eyes closed, feeling the energy of the earth beneath you.

Squats

Yes! I know it may sound a bit weird, but I do squats every morning as a part of my morning ritual and as a quick home workout. They give me a great energy boost and I feel so much better for the rest of the day. Usually, I do some squats first and then a few mini sun salutations. Sometimes I may add some more exercises or do a meditation, it depends on how much time I've got, but this is my usual morning routine before I jump into the shower.

So...try some squats now. Stand with your feet comfortably apart. Bend your knees and assume a squatting position, taking care to keep your feet flat on the floor. Do this for one to three minutes. Something that may also help would be to get involved in sports and activities that promote balance.

Body Work

Taking care of your health will ease the burden from your root chakra and make it function better. Meditation calms down negative thoughts and emotions, which will allow you to focus on other things aside from psychological survival. Simply sit down, close your eyes, breathe, and observe what's happening. Don't try to change anything. It's OK to have some thoughts, but focus on accepting them and tell your subconscious that this is your sacred time to feel grounded and secure. Nobody wants anything, nobody needs anything. Simply sit down, breathe, and relax.

Physical movements such as those in sports and exercise bring attention back to the body and help an underactive root chakra. This grounding effect is heightened when done outdoors in the presence of nature, so try to be outside as much as possible. Our busy modern lifestyles and sedentary office jobs make it a bit hard to follow this guideline, but outside of work, you should still have some free hours that you can use to re-balance yourself. Instead of getting glued to another screen (like a tablet, phone, TV, or laptop), make a conscious decision to go out and fuel your body and mind with the smell, sound, and feeling of nature.

Because the root chakra's element is earth, anything that involves earth and its derivatives may help boost and regulate it. Simply walking on the ground barefoot or going hiking every now and then may also do the trick because it reconnects the body with the earth.

Energy work

Bring your attention to your first chakra by seeing it in your body or by picturing it on a 'mental screen' outside of you – either way will work fine as long as you have the intention of working with it. Give it the shape that you want. Whatever feels right for you. What and how do you want your chakra to be? Strong red? Pulsating? Energizing light? Keep an open mind and observe. What can you notice about it?

Mindset Change (the most important in my humble opinion)

The first chakra's fight or flight reflex stems from the spirit's own tendency to protect itself. Like the body, the soul doesn't like pain. If survival issues are not managed, the spirit may not want to experience life. To deal with this, it's important to remember that the soul is incarnated to gain benefits. It must not escape from the experiences that our existence has to offer.

Being independent is also a focus of the first chakra. Depending on your own self is an achievement of a properly functioning root chakra. Reflect on whether you are depending on other people too much. On the other hand, be careful if you are driven to help other people at the expense of your own comfort. Not only are you denying yourself of self-care, but you may also cause others to become too dependent on you, which may lead their root chakras to weaken. Strive for balance in helping and being helped. In order to help others, you must first help yourself.

Natural Remedies

Herbs: Raspberry leaf, cloves, ginseng, dandelion root

Sound Therapy

Meditating on the C note attunes the chakra to its frequency.

Chapter 2 - Day 2 - The Second Chakra. Embracing Healthy Pleasures of Life

The second chakra is the sacral chakra located at a height between the pubic area and the navel. It's centered on emotions, desires, and relationships. Because it is associated with the sexual organs, it is said to be responsible for the sexual drive as well. An overactive sacral chakra equals an overactive libido that is hard to control and verges on obsession. Likewise, an underactive sacral chakra provokes unusually low libido.

Creativity is also linked to this chakra because of its association with the reproductive organs. You symbolically give birth to whatever you're creating, whether it's writing, cooking, raising your kids, making clothes, or even doing your hair.

If you go back to Maslow's hierarchy mentioned in the previous chapter, you will see that this chakra is related to the third classification of needs – love and belongingness. The fourth chakra also deals with love and connection to other people, but the second chakra deals with the lower expressions of love – arousal, infatuation, the desire for approval, the drive to seek pleasure, etc.

Emotions are perceived and processed through the second chakra. Think about this chakra like water. In fact, this chakra is actually associated with the element of water. The energy of this chakra flows within and around us. It spills over and yearns for things and people that lie outside of us. From this chakra, you learn how to connect with others and know how and when to form boundaries.

Emotional Imbalances

Too much or too little emotion could be a sign of a troubled sacral chakra. The sacral chakra's action of blending boundaries (as represented by sex) can also become problematic. It can manifest as attachment and manipulation, which result to difficult relationships. A sacral chakra imbalance can also be felt as excessive guilt when experiencing pleasure.

Too much sacral energy can result in addictions and compulsions. Too little of it may provoke disinterest and repression.

Affirmations

- I am in touch with my emotions
- I am creative
- I know how to express my emotions
- I eat healthy foods that help me feel balanced
- I am good at making decisions
- I feel good about myself
- I love healthy activities that bring me closer to my goals and make me feel good
- I am valuable
- I control how I feel
- I allow myself to feel alive
- I am comfortable with my sexuality
- I respect other people's feelings

Incantations

Lam

Yoga and Other Balancing Exercises

-Mudra

Rest your hands upon your lap. Place your hands on top of each other (the right resting on the left), with the palms facing upwards. Align your hands in such a way that you can connect the tips of your thumbs together.

-All yoga exercises that involve hip movement help you balance the sacral chakra. Its corresponding body parts are the sexual organs, the lower back, hips, and lower abdomen.

-Belly and Chest Breathing

Sit cross-legged or lie down. Place your palms on your belly slightly below your navel. Inhale and exhale slowly while feeling your stomach rise and fall. Concentrate on the sacral chakra as you breathe this way for a couple of minutes.

-Goddess Pose

Stand with your legs as far apart as possible with your knees bent at a 90° angle, the inner part of your thighs facing forward. Put your arms out to the side, and bend them upwards at the elbows.

-Sitting Position

Sit with your back straight. Press the soles of your feet together in front of you. Let the outer portion of your legs and thighs touch the floor. Do this for a couple of minutes.

Butter Fly Pose

-Body Work

Doing anything enjoyable and safe will help balance your sacral chakra. For example: relaxing, going to a spa, listening to music, being intimate with a loving partner, etc. Because the sacral chakra involves sensations and feelings, any activity that involves the emotions and senses will also invigorate a depleted sacral chakra.

While doing something pleasurable, get in touch with the sensations you're having and allow your feelings to surface to awareness. Do not block yourself from pleasure; allow yourself to become immersed.

Energy Work

-As with the previous chakra, you need to be in tune with your sacral chakra in order to work with it. Observe the chakra and receive impressions of what's coming from it. Ask the chakra about what you need to know from it. Do this for a few minutes until you feel ready to move on to the next part of the process.

-Ask your chakra: am I repressing anything? Am I addicted to anything? Be silent and pay attention. The responses may come in images, thoughts, or memories. Record these if you're able to.

-This chakra may be blocked by guilt or repressed desires. If the desire is safe and appropriate, indulge in it. If it is something that you would rather not do no matter how badly you want it, just accept it at this point. Acknowledging the desire will help diffuse its potency. Feel the desire without criticizing it or adding energy to it. Understand its nature and what it is trying to make you do. When you notice that the desire is getting stronger, take deep breaths, relax, and empty your thoughts. You may choose to do another thing which is more acceptable than the desire. This will help to expel the energy that is stuck in the sacral chakra.

-You may cleanse yourself of negative energy by draining it from your chakra. Imagine the stuck energy passing from your body through a cord that's connected to the ground. Affirm that the blockage is being removed.

-Imagine that you are happy and that you accept your desires. How does it make you feel? How does that thought affect the quality of your sacral chakra? Allow yourself to become blissful. This will not only heal your sacral chakra, but it will boost your entire energetic level as well.

Other Activities

-Write a letter of gratitude

-Swim, go to the beach, spend some time immersed in the ocean, a lake, river, or even in a pool or a bathtub. Adding some essential oils to your bath, like the ones recommended in this chapter can help you soothe negative emotions, but a word of caution: dilute your essential oils in some vegetable oil, just as you would for massage.

-Accept the feelings of guilt

-Meditate chanting the sound: *VAM*

-Aromatherapy

Use rose, jasmine, bergamot, verbena, cedar wood, cinnamon, or ylang ylang essential oils

Just like I mentioned earlier, you can use them for self-massage (making sure to blend them with a quality base oil, for example: coconut oil). Focus on the area below your navel and lower back.

Mindset Change

Emotions are bundles of energy that are meant to flow. If you keep them stuck deep inside you, they might cause damage to you both physically and psychologically. Release them. Express them in a creative way. For example, anger can be let go of while sweating in a gym, while sadness can be transmuted into poetry in your journal. You may also consider kick boxing classes or any other type of martial arts. Kick it out and shout it out. Go for a quick run or do a fitness class to sweat it out. The sooner those negative emotions are out of your body, the more health you will attract. Negative emotions that get stuck in your chakras may lead to physical diseases and imbalances. This is one of the fundamental philosophies of holistic medicine- your mental and emotional health may affect your physical wellness.

Emotions are powerful because they cause you to do things according to your needs. They are usually simple and program-like in the sense that they activate because of a trigger. They cause you to do things to meet a certain goal that will benefit you in some way. To gain control over these mini-programs, look at the experience intellectually. Determine the emotion, its trigger, and its consequences. Break the link between them using the following methods:

- decide to act differently when the trigger arises
- evade the triggers
- do not take immediate action when you feel an unwanted emotion
- simply feel the emotion without adding strength to it until it fades away
- relax your body and mind to diffuse the potency of the feeling

- be aware of negative emotions that you are prone to and keep asking yourself "why"

Natural Remedies

-Drinking natural liquids such as water, carrot, and orange juices. I recommend you mix them with some water. Herbal teas will soothe an imbalanced sacral chakra. Avoid caffeine - it will aggravate any negative emotions you may have, whether it's anger or worry. The way that media markets coffee is very often, "Relax, have a cup of coffee," but it works the other way around. It triggers more anger that you already have in yourself. It's better to relax with caffeine-free infusions like fennel (my favorite), mint, rosemary, or Melissa.

-Use cinnamon, maca powder, or ginger. You can add them into your smoothies. Maca is a natural remedy for low libido.

***Of course, remember that certain imbalances that are reflected in a low libido or total withdrawal from sexual activities are more of a mental and emotional nature. For example, someone who has been raped or has experienced any similar trauma should not be afraid to seek professional help and therapy. Hypnotherapy can help to build a new foundation and get rid of past traumas, as are Reiki and Bach

Flower remedies. I believe that the most important thing is to know what event has caused such an imbalance.

On the other hand, many modern people who complain about low libido find that it is mainly due to 2 factors: not enough nutrition and lack of communication with their partner or spouse. Getting away for a few days and reducing the amount of time spent in front of a screen or even booking a short vacation together can help. Slowing down a bit, getting more involved in sports, relaxation, and eating a balanced diet (simply eat clean, eliminate processed crap that only serves to mess up your hormones, and add more fresh fruits and vegetables into your diet) can also help restore one's libido.

Crystals

-Use orange crystals (ex. carnelian, tiger's eye)

Keep them on or near your meditation mat or carry one around with you. You can also keep it on your nightstand.

Sound Therapy

Meditating on the D note attunes the chakra to this frequency.

Chapter 3 - Day 3 - The Third Chakra. You Deserve to Be Confident

The third chakra is called the solar plexus chakra. It is located at your solar plexus, the area at the midpoint of your chest where your ribcage connects. Its Sanskrit name is Manipura (meaning diamond). It is linked with willpower, self-esteem and personal identity. It powers a person's assertiveness, decisiveness, and motivation. This chakra assists you in setting your own path in life.

If you have ever experienced anxiety, I would venture to say that you had some kind of imbalances in this very chakra. And I am with you. Working on this chakra is my main focus now. Even though I have made lots of progress and let many things go, I still have certain amount self-work to do. It's still a journey for me!

You see, if you are an ambitious person, like me, and if at certain point you let your ambitions take control of you, you may get to the point where you become a workaholic, getting obsessed about your career or even about your personal development. I myself was too obsessed about chakras which actually, instead of helping me, aggravated my anxiety at one stage. The key lesson I learned was that I had to embrace self-love and self-care. I had to understand where the limits were so that I could carry on with my work without letting it take control of me and take my emotional wellness away.

Luckily, workaholism is pretty easy to cure. Most people reach the "seekers" stage when they try to explore natural therapies and find fulfillment in themselves rather than in what they accomplish. Of course, it's important to move forward with your ambitions and goals, and I am all for it, but health and emotional wellbeing should never be the price for success.

Working on your body, mind, and spirit is great, and this is what I promote. However, a healthy balance is needed so that you don't get too obsessed. Another lesson to learn is to avoid judgment when you see people who are not on the same journey as you are. But you see, judging them would be the same as judging yourself from a few years ago. There are no timelines for the Universe, so in a sense, if you are judging your friends because they have a different lifestyle, you are judging and maybe even hating yourself. Bad combination! The feeling you may get is this burning sensation or even pain in your solar plexus.

You see, the main theme of this chakra is your personal power – knowing who you really are, where you are going, and making full use of what you have. This power gives you the courage to experience life in all its ups and downs.

The solar plexus chakra regulates the way that energy is directed through the body, so it is also connected to the way you direct your attention and energy. It is possible that you will use this power in controlling more than just yourself, but other people as well. A healthy solar plexus makes you strong in the sense that you are comfortable with life and you do not have to dominate others in order to be happy.

Imbalances: I have mostly focused on what happens if this chakra is overactive, however there is also the other side of the spectrum. An unbalanced solar plexus chakra may encourage feelings of insecurity in a person. He or she may either become hypersensitive, or become ruthless in order to make up for his or her insecurities. There may also be an obsession toward status.

Over-activity in the solar chakra creates a personality that is both domineering because of excessive drive to direct things, and narrow-minded because of the nature of the solar plexus to place importance to one's own self and views.

Under-activity in the solar chakra can lead to submissiveness, compulsivity, and foolishness because of a lack of willpower.

Affirmations

- I am strong
- I have a healthy self-esteem
- I radiate my power
- I can withstand the challenges that come my way
- I love expressing my emotions
- I am sensitive
- I believe in myself
- If there is no way, I will make a way
- I trust the Universal energy
- I am focused
- I am productive
- I only focus on what's necessary in my journey
- I listen to my inner voice
- I release my fears and struggles effortlessly

- I am good at solving problems
- I am good at learning new things
- Challenges make me grow
- I let go of everything I no longer need, including past traumas and negative emotions
- I am friendly, joyful, and confident
- I accept other people
- I listen to my body and I know when to slow down
- I give my body and mind what they need
- I am happy
- I don't worry about what others think about me
- I follow my own choices
- I am responsible
- I create my destiny

Balancing Activities and Hobbies

-Laugh more often.

-Spend time with animals. I personally love cats, there's so much to learn from them!

-Be like a curious little kid, jump around, touch and feel everything you can

-Cry if you feel you need to, let the tears out. Many men think that crying is something that "real men should never do."

Wrong! There is nothing wrong with a man who needs to cry, just like there is nothing wrong with a man who cooks, cleans, or treats himself to facials.

-Painting, drawing, and photography.

-Enjoying the sunshine.

-Sitting by the fire or meditating with a candle.

-Spending more time outdoors.

-Always celebrate your successes and achievements, even the smallest milestones.

-Try taking up new activities and hobbies.

-Spend more time doing things that you enjoy. In my case it's going to the beach. I actually added it to my lifestyle goals: go to the beach 2-3 times a week. What balances me is sunshine and water. Even though I could work a few hours more, ever since I got committed to going to the beach, more ideas started pouring in and I was able to focus better and accomplish more work in less time. When you feel good, you work better! To me, the beach is like a temple, a natural spa. I also like the woods that are a 2-minute walk from my house, but this summer I made a commitment of going to the beach 2-3 times a week. For now, I have been getting great results. In addition, I combine it with yoga, fitness, walking in the sand, swimming, and even writing. Like I said before, the beach really inspires me.

So what is your beach? What is your soothing inspiration? Do you deprive yourself of doing things you enjoy because you want to play a superhero and be in your office every day, or maybe you think you don't deserve it or are too lazy or indecisive to choose what works for you? All of these things are limiting beliefs, and your task now is to try to get rid of them. Be a little kid again. Design your ideal day to energize your body and mind. Your solar plexus chakra needs some extra power. In this day and age, I think that solar chakra imbalances are really common. On a physical level they manifest themselves in digestive problems. I think most of us have been there, right?

So what's the solution?

It's simplicity! Less technology, more sunshine. More touch. More creativity, more curiosity, and sometimes even more effort. For those of you whose solar chakra is overactive, I would suggest less undertakings and professional activities. This doesn't mean you have to get lazy, you just need to learn to slow down. I talk about it in my book "Holistically Productive" that you can download for free from my blog, www.HolisticWellnessProject.com

The question you need to ask yourself is, "Am I overactive or underactive? Is my challenge doing more, or doing less?"

Incantations

Ram

Yoga

-Mudra

Place your hands between your belly and heart. Connect the tips of your hand's index, middle, ring, and pinky finger to those of your other hand's. Make your thumbs cross and overlap each other. Holding this position, place the base of your palm against your navel area.

-The abdomen is the main body part connected to the solar plexus. Anything that involves the belly and abdominal muscles can stimulate the solar plexus chakra.

-Solar Meditation

Sit or stand with your arms stretching to the sky in a V position. Imagine that the energy of the sun is reaching you and penetrating your being. Inhale the golden light and exhale the shadows within you.

-Bow Pose

Lie on your stomach with your chin touching on the floor. Bend both legs and bring your heels up onto your buttocks. Inhale deeply. As you exhale, pull up the muscles of your abdomen. Inhale and slowly lift your head and feet. Squeeze your shoulder blades together. Carefully rock back and forth with each breath for 10 seconds.

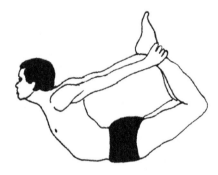

-Boat Pose

Sit on the floor. Grab the back of your thighs. Inhale and lean back with your toes still in contact with the floor. When you exhale, pull your stomach in. Hold the pose for a few seconds.

Body Work

-The solar plexus is considered as a person's seat of power. Any activity that allows him or her to exert energy will work on this chakra. Invigorating activities such as competitive sports, swimming, aerobics, and challenging sports are ideal for balancing the solar plexus.

-Pilates deals with the core muscles of the abdomen. Take up Pilates exercises to increase your solar plexus power.

Energy Work

Check your solar plexus chakra. Some issues to concentrate on are:

-Are you trying to influence something or somebody too much? If the answer is yes, who are these people or situations?

-Are there people or situations that are trampling on you? Who or what are they?

These things drain your solar plexus energy. Separate these from yourself through visualizing and resolving to distance yourself from them in your day-to-day life.

Imagine that you are no longer connected to those things that sap your energy. What is it like? Is it a better experience than being stuck with issues that stifle your growth? If the answer is yes, accept that you may have to let go of these things. Instead of focusing on how losing them might feel, center your attention on how good running on your own energy will feel like.

Aromatherapy

Chamomile, peppermint, rose, sweet orange, mandarin, tea tree, and sandalwood

My recommendation - blend your chosen oil (about 5 drops) in 1 tablespoon of a vegetable oil (for example coconut) and massage your solar plexus. Breathe deeply in and out. Enjoy the aromas. It's a great time to practice your affirmations, like for example, "I am confident."

Mindset Change

-When you exercise your willpower, you also deal with the energies of the solar plexus. Deliberately strengthen your resolve by choosing a goal and sticking to it no matter what challenges and distractions may come your way. You don't need to choose a very difficult goal, something as simple as writing with your non-dominant hand or not saying swear words will be enough.

-If you are prone to controlling other people, first reflect on what you are compensating for. Those who have the need to dictate external people and events are often those who feel anxious about things not going their way. What are you afraid of? What can you let go of so that you will be more accepting of life and situations that you can't control?

-Confronting your fears will loosen up congested energy in your solar plexus. Hypnotherapists can help you with this. One technique for shedding a phobia is this:

Remember the last time that you encountered the subject of your fear. Relive the experience vividly – recreate what you were thinking, feeling, and doing at that time. Then, take deep breaths and imagine that the experience was something you are watching from a movie screen. Freeze it. Now, it's time to reduce the effect of the memory on you. You do this by changing the memory's characteristics. Drain it of color and turn it into black and white. Mute the sound. You can also turn the horror film into comedy by making the characters act silly or by adding funny sounds. When you change the dominant emotion of fear, feel a sense of relief in yourself. Then, run the entire clip backwards until it stops and nothing remains within your view. Do this a lot of times. Soon, the memory will have reshaped itself and it will no longer produce the same debilitating effects as before.

Natural Remedies

-Foods made of complex carbohydrates (grains like quinoa, legumes, seeds, and nuts)

-Foods rich in magnesium like, for example, bananas

Crystals

 -Yellow crystals (ex. citrine, yellow topaz)

You can use them to rub your solar plexus or simply lie down on your back and place your chosen crystal on your chest.

Sound Therapy

-Meditating on the E note attunes the chakra to this frequency.

Chapter 4 - Day 4 - The Fourth Chakra - Love Yourself and the Universe. Love Will Set You Free!

Everyone wants to love and be loved, right? The question is, are you connected to the force of the Universal love? Do you love yourself?

It's time to move up your spine and explore the next chakra. The fourth chakra. It's called the heart chakra (*Anahata* in Sanscrit which means "unstruck") and it is positioned at the heart. It is the midpoint of the 7 chakras. It is a neutral place where you can work on yourself and your relationships with other people.

Like the second chakra, the fourth chakra is also a center of emotions but it is focused mainly on higher emotions such as love, devotion, and kindness. The sacral chakra is geared towards the pursuit of selfish pleasure, while the heart chakra is capable of demonstrating selfless love. It integrates the insights of the lower chakras and provides a wider perspective on them. When you function with your heart chakra, you will begin to view yourself as a part of a whole. This allows you to see the bigger picture, which is calming and centering.

If you balance your heart chakra, you will take care of your emotional health, release anxiety, improve your current relationships, and find people who are loving and compassionate as well. Some say that working on the heart chakra may also help you find your soul mate. I believe there may be some truth in that because by working on this chakra, you cultivate self-love and self-acceptance. All relationship experts claim that in order to have a happy and fulfilling relationship, you must first love yourself.

So what happens if this chakra is imbalanced?

The typical symptoms of *Anahata* not receiving enough love are:
Heartaches or lack of emotion. Those who deny their feelings may likewise cause their heart chakra to suffer. Anger and sadness are common emotions for this disorder.

Because the heart chakra provides a connection between a person and those around him or her, imbalances will affect how he or she relates with them. A balanced heart chakra promotes relationships that are based on love and compassion, while an imbalanced heart chakra will breed problematic relationships. It might also result in the person's refusal to reach out to others. It might also provide him or her with a twisted sense of what love is.

The heart chakra is very interesting because it's like a middle chakra. There are 3 chakras underneath it and 3 above it. It is like a meeting point. It mixes the lower chakras (our relationships with society) with the upper chakras (those that deal with your connection to the divine and creating a soulful life).

Affirmations

- I allow myself to receive and give love
- I help others
- I ask for help when I need it
- I open myself to the people around me
- I love freely and happily
- I am ready to receive happiness from my relationships
- I am empathic towards myself and others
- I am driven by contribution
- I am selfless

- I am aware of my energy
- I deeply and truly love and accept myself
- I forgive myself and others
- I believe in love
- I deserve true love
- Love is the answer to all of my worries
- Love is everywhere
- My heart is full of love and compassion
- I can heal myself and others
- I welcome the differences of others
- I am grateful for my life and people I have attracted
- I believe in everything that I do
- I accept myself and others

Recommended Activities to Balance This Chakra:

-Practice cardio exercises, yoga, and breathing techniques to help strengthen your physical heart. Eat a healthy diet full of fresh fruits and vegetables, nuts, and seeds. Healthy fats, lean proteins, and good carbs like, for example, quinoa.

-Read books on spirituality and personal development. Actually, this is what you are doing now. You are a seeker, so good job, keep going, keep exploring, and don't forget to apply what you have learned.

-Go outside more often, because this chakra is associated with air. Have a walk in a park or on the beach and feel the wind on your face. It's healing and refreshing.

-Take up hobbies that you feel you are good at.

-Add more greens into your diet. Since I love the alkaline diet and lifestyle, this is my favorite thing to do. Now, some say it's a placebo effect, but those who drink green, chlorophyll-rich juices and smoothies very often report the feeling of connectedness, and even a natural high and boosted energy. I have experienced it myself many times. Even if the mental and emotional benefits of green drinks are placebo effects, on a physical level, adding more greens into your diet will help you maintain a healthy pH in your blood and eliminate toxins from your body. Both physical and emotional toxins should always be eliminated as frequently as possible!

-If you feel lost, reach out to a coach, mentor, or therapist. There is nothing wrong with asking for help, we all have our ups and downs. It all comes down to coming up with solutions that help us feel better. Ask other people for guidance if you need it.

-Treat yourself to regular massage and Reiki treatments. Self-care is self-love. You can also spoil yourself with aromatherapy self-massage, aromatherapy baths, and create your holistic home spa. You can check out my book "Wellness Treatments" if you need a few more ideas.

-Add more green color into your life, maybe even start wearing it more often.

Incantations

Yam

Yoga

-Mudra

Link the index finger and thumb of each hand so that you form two small circles with them. Put one hand on your left knee and the other on the middle of your chest.

-The center of the chest is the best spot for heart chakra exercises.

-Cobra Pose

Lie face down with your chin upon the floor. Keep your feet together and point your toes back. Place your palms parallel to your chin with your elbows bent. Inhale and lift your upper body off the floor while raising your head, chest and shoulders. Your lower body must remain on the floor. Lengthen your neck and tuck in your chin. Inhale and exhale slowly 5 times. On exhaling, lower your upper body. Breathe.

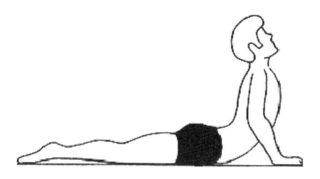

-Fish Pose

Lie on your back and bend your knees. Keep the back of your heels on the floor. Inhale and raise your pelvis slightly. Slide both hands' palm down beneath your buttocks. Exhale. Inhale and press your arms against the ground. Lift your chest.

-Cow Head

Sit with your shoulders relaxed. Reach your left palm behind you and touch the center of your back. Raise your right arm next to your right ear. Reach over the right shoulder and lock fingers of both hands. Hold for 10 seconds.

-Crystals

Use green herderite, pink danburite, rose quartz, aventurine, jade, or petalite.

Body Work

-Actions that spark loving emotions are good for the heart chakra, especially if it includes being kind to others. Helping other people through charity work, interacting with loved ones, and participating in an inspirational experience are just some of the things you can do for heart chakra balancing.

Energy Work

-Close your eyes and relax. Really focus and zoom in to your heart chakra. Explore this chakra like a room – notice details and record them if you are able to. Do you perceive love in that space? Do you see any people or things in there? What are they doing? How are you reacting towards them?

-Clean the room of your heart by sweeping off negative emotions. You may change the furniture arrangement and decor if you wish, in order to create a more loving atmosphere. Shine a bright green light into your heart with the intention of healing your heart and yourself.

-Do you have blockages in your heart chakra? You can blast them off by creating energy tools with your imagination. You can imagine a golden net to filter out the negative energy particles or a flamethrower to incinerate stubborn blockages. Suck it away with a vacuum cleaner with a built-in incinerator inside. Although these may seem like make-believe to you, it will still affect your mind in such a way that it will help you process negative emotions better.

Mindset Change

-Love can take on many forms – friendly love, romantic love, sacrificial love, or intellectual love. There's nothing wrong with love, but the way it is expressed can be harmful to a person. Reflect on the way you feel love and manifest it. What do you think about love? What feelings, beliefs, and memories do you link with it? Once you have clarified these, ask yourself: is it worthwhile to keep them, or do you need to change them into something more beneficial to you?

-True love is empowering. It is not manipulative or self-destructive. What is keeping you from experiencing the best that love has to offer? Is it because you were made to believe that you are not worthy enough, or that no one can be trusted with love? Realize that these beliefs may be faulty and check whether they're causing you more harm than good. Be willing to let go of these notions in favor of those that serve you.

-Open your heart. You will find love when you become loving yourself. The more you experience love in your heart, the easier it will be for you to perceive it around you. Take courage and be the first to turn on the light in your heart.

How to Find Your Soul Mate

-Soul mates are connected to each other no matter how great the distance between them may be. By meditating on these subtle connections, you will increase their strength and you can gently tug your soul mate closer to you.

-Imagine that within your heart is a golden thread that leads to your partner. Visualize that person in front of you. Tell him or her that you are ready for your soul mate to appear in your life. Send loving energies his or her way, and have faith that the Universe is now working towards bringing you back together.

Aromatherapy

Use essential oils as neroli, rose, or marjoram. I recommend mindful chest massage with one of these oils. Breathe in deeply and focus on your affirmations

Natural Remedies

-Green vegetables are not only good for the physical heart, but for the heart chakra as well, and so are green supplements. For example, my favorite, alfalfa powder.

-Drink jasmine tea. It will give you the feeling of a "natural high" and connectedness with the here and now. It will help you relax, energizing your mind while purifying your body and energy field at the same time.

Sound Therapy

Meditating on the F note attunes the chakra to this frequency.

More Tips

-When you find yourself judging others (nobody is perfect, we all do it), first of all accept it. Don't beat yourself up. Breathe into your heart on an inhale and on the exhale, just let the judgment go, imagining it's a dark cloud leaving your body. Then, call out the name of the person you were judging and say to yourself, "I am sorry. Even though I have judged this person, I accept it and I will still try to let it go."

-Try to spend some time alone, even just in your thoughts, and reflect upon your behavior. Enjoy your company, be your best friend!

-When journaling ask yourself:

Do you seek approval and acceptance? If so, from whom, why, and when?

How would it feel if you knew nobody would ever judge you?

Would you be content to know that you don't care about what others think or say about you?

Chapter 5 - Day 5 - Throat Chakra - Express Yourself and Create Personal Success

The throat chakra (Vishudda) is related to self-expression and communication. It supports our ability to receive, process, and share our knowledge. This chakra is traditionally linked with sound, but it's interesting that this is confirmed by modern studies. According to new research, having an internal dialogue lights up areas of the brain that are associated with sound, and it can also make the muscles of your throat move even if you don't intend to move them. Body and mind connection, right?

Imbalances

An inability to express one's thoughts is one of the marks of an underdeveloped throat chakra. A hyperactive one may cause a person to become a motor-mouth or be verbally abusive to other people.

When this chakra is balanced, you are able to speak and live the truth. What does that mean? It's simple: your actions are congruent with your real passions. You decide to achieve your goals, not someone else's goals. You are connected with your inner self.

Affirmations

- I am able to express myself freely
- I am motivated to know and tell the truth
- I speak clearly and fluently
- I am in control of my thoughts
- I am confident with the things that I know
- I hear the truth
- I speak the truth
- I express myself with clear intent
- My inner voice is strong
- Creativity flows in and through me
- It is correct and safe for me to be able to express my true essence
- I enjoy being myself
- I am artistic
- I love listening
- I love public speaking
- My words both help and inspire other people

Remember, this chakra is happy when what you say matches up to who you really are. It's time to start a journey to self-authenticity...

Balancing Activities

-Meditate while looking at the sky or ocean

-Add more blue into your life in the form of clothes, or things around your house

-Add more herbal teas, organic honey, soups, vegetable creams, and fresh vegetable juices into your diet. They will help to lubricate the mouth and throat. If you take care of yourself on a physical level, your chakras will really appreciate it. Of course, there is also some inner work to do. You already know all about it and you can't wait to proceed to more balancing activities, right?

-Add fruits like lemon, lime, kiwi, grapefruit, pears, peaches, and apricots into your diet. Smoothies are also a great way to add both fruits and vegetables into your diet.

-Dance, sing, and don't be afraid to be more creative with the way you dress yourself and do your hair. As long as you like it, you are good to go!

-Listening to pleasant music can be good for the throat chakra because of its relation to sound. In particular, classical music can also boost the intelligence, while meditative music can help calm the mind. The sound of nature and uplifting noises (for example children laughing or the kettle whistling) will also be effective.

Incantations

Ham

Yoga

- Mudra

Bring your two hands together at the level of your stomach, palms up, and interlace your fingers. Press your thumbs together to create a large circle with both of your hands.

-The neck and throat areas are linked to the throat chakra. By focusing on these areas, you will also exert an energetic influence on the chakra.

-Shoulder Shrugs

Inhale and bring your shoulders toward your ears. Exhale and allow your shoulders to descend and relax into their original positions. Do this in rhythm with your breath for about a minute or so. Next, bend your elbows and place your fingertips on your shoulders. Inhale and rotate your elbows, circling 5 times forward. Exhale and rotate your elbows in the opposite direction for another 5 times.

-Bridge Pose

Lie on the floor. Bend your legs at the knees so that your feet rest flat on the floor. Stretch out your arms towards your feet with the palms pressing down the ground. Slowly lift your lower body off the ground but keep your head, neck, and shoulder blades in contact with the floor.

-Camel Pose

Kneel on the ground. Carefully reach back and hold on to your heels. Keep this position for as long as you can.

Body Work

Using your voice serves two purposes. It both exercises and unblocks the throat chakra. This can be things like talking with friends, delivering a speech, chanting mantras, or singing songs. Anything that involves creative expression is also related to the throat chakra and will influence it. Writing poetry, painting, playing music, and performing will help as well.

Energy Work

-Imagine that you can see your throat chakra. What does it look like? Is it big or small? Is it moving rapidly or sluggishly? Does it have dirt or smoke in it?

-Imagine that you are inside your throat chakra. You have become smaller and the chakra is as big as a hallway. What do you experience around you? It's possible that you might hear things because this chakra is involved with sound and thoughts. Take note of them.

-You may see people and scenarios around you. Watch if these are benefitting you or harming you. Are they keeping you from being true to yourself? Have you allowed them to impose their own truths upon you, to the point that you have repressed your own reality? Clean the negative energy in this chakra by illuminating it with brilliant blue light.

Aromatherapy

-Use chamomile, rosemary, lemongrass (I am actually using lemongrass right now, I love it when I am writing it's very body and mind invigorating), geranium, sage, or hyssop

Mindset Change

-The fifth chakra is all about expressing what is true for you. Are you bottling your thoughts up inside of yourself? Are you pretending to be someone you're not? The mind craves congruency because it takes a lot of energy to maintain processes that contradict each other. In simple words, it's easier for your mind if you behave in line with what you really believe. Spare yourself the stress by upholding your truth and acting in accordance with it.

-Remember that everyone has the right to self-expression. If you're afraid to loosen up, ask yourself if that fear is valid. Imagine that you have succeeded in opening up – how does it feel? What may have happened? You may realize that your hesitation is caused by dreaming up things that will not happen in reality. Confront these illusions by finding as much as you can, and resolving to act on the information you gather.

-Do you need help in sorting things out? You can seek the help of a counselor. Otherwise, research more, analyze the things you learn, and test what you know through application.

Learning logic and critical thinking will help you immensely because these two subjects are all about figuring out the truth.

-A clear focus is one sign of a healthy throat chakra. If you're having problems concentrating, consider meditating daily. A simple form of meditation is to focus on your breathing for 15-20 minutes. Whenever you notice that your attention is drifting away, just go back to noticing your inhalations and exhalations. If you do this daily, you will train your mind to refocus itself on whatever you need to focus on.

-You can set the focus of your day by using a planner. Write down what you need to do for the day and check what you have accomplished. Do this every morning before you leave your bedroom. The mind is like a butterfly that floats from flower to flower. Give your mind a map (the to-do list) to streamline its efforts and make it accomplish more. Make sure not to get hung up on the details, though. Limit planning time to no more than 20 minutes a day, then drop the pen, and act on those plans. Planning and doing things will free up the load that's on your mind and make you do more things. It's like having a mental shower.

Natural Remedies

-The fifth chakra is connected to air, thus fruits that are picked from trees will resonate with it

-Use spices like lemongrass and pink Himalayan salt

Crystals

Use blue colored crystals (aquamarine, sapphire, tourmaline, blue calcite). Place them on your throat chakra or get a necklace that will always protect you.

Sound Therapy

Meditating on the C note attunes the chakra to this frequency.

Chapter 6 - Day 6 - Third Eye Chakra - Embrace Your Intuition and Let It Guide You in Your Spiritual Enlightenment

The sixth chakra is well-known as the third eye chakra. For some people it may sound like some kind of pseudo-scientific or spiritual hocus pocus, but read on with an open mind. Analyze your situation and ask yourself a few questions. This chakra helps you see the world in a certain way, think of it as a pair of glasses that either help you see things as they are and recognize the truth, or glasses that don't fit and give you a distorted image of what you see. You may also think of it as glasses of positivity or negativity. As an eye, it provides not only psychic sight but also normal sight as well. Although some chakra and aura experts say that even if you physical eye sight is not perfect (for example those of you who are short-sighted like me who need glasses or lenses), your intuitive and Universal eye may still be functioning perfectly. However, eye conditions, infections, and diseases may be the sign that something is wrong with this chakra, which was my case when I suffered from uveitis.

The sixth chakra is located slightly above the midpoint of the two eyes. It is said that the pineal gland is the physical counterpart of this chakra, and this gland does seem to be an eye because it has light-sensitive receptors on it. Other than that, it also secretes DMT, a substance known to cause visions and other mystical experiences.

The third eye chakra brings illumination and understanding. It is said to be the place where we can tap into divine wisdom.

Imbalances

The effects of an imbalanced third eye chakra are the inability to use intuition and psychic abilities. Confusion, lack of direction, poor memory, insomnia, eye conditions, and learning disabilities may also be a result of this imbalance. On the other side of the spectrum, if this chakra is too active, you may find yourself living in a fantasy world and having a problem with accepting reality. This is not good either. We want a balance in this chakra so that our conscious and unconscious minds are connected and work for us and our holistic wellness.

Affirmations

- I am seeing clearly
- I am thinking well
- I am connected to the divine
- I am an infinite being
- I trust my intuition
- I love the world
- I accept the truth
- I accept what I see
- I am grateful for my eyesight
- I learn from all experiences, both good and bad
- I can visualize my future clearly
- I see everything clearly
- I follow my dreams and my visions
- I believe in my dreams
- I live a life of purpose
- I have a strong vision
- I am creative
- I create my life
- I follow my inner voice
- I remember my dreams
- I love dreaming
- I have a vivid and powerful imagination
- I am open to spiritual awareness
- I explore my spirituality

Balancing Activities

-Spend time in non-competitive sports, and do exercises that will also help you work with your energy, like yoga, walking meditation, tai chi, qigong, visualization, and chanting mantras

-Give yourself some time to recharge your batteries and give your mind a break

-Take care of your eyesight. If you spend a lot of time working in front of a PC, make sure to take regular breaks

-Switch off technology and don't get too obsessed about your mobile devices, and in addition, reduce your internet time. This may be a bit hard at first, but in the end, it'll be worth it

-Avoid social situations that you know will totally drain you. If these cannot be avoided, make sure you meditate before and after and use affirmations I suggested above to replenish this chakra and make it work for you and protect you

-Involve yourself in activities that help you improve your memory

-Seek the help of a coach or mentor so that they can give you honest feedback about your actions and thoughts. You see, we very often need to understand and embrace a real image of ourselves. That image very often, due to our own perceptions and limiting beliefs, may be distorted. A coach, therapist, or even a spiritual advisor can help you so that you are more connected to your spirit and your true self instead of your ego, which is your false self

-Don't over-intellectualize, over-do, or over-think things. In this day and age when there is so much information to absorb, it's pretty difficult. Information overload can actually prevent you from taking action. A simple example: imagine a person who wants to lose weight and is searching for "the best" diet. They come across at least 20 different diets and programs and feel lost. They don't know what to choose, they feel paralyzed. I always suggest baby steps. Take one tiny thing that you can stick to and try it. If it doesn't work, change the strategy, if it does work, amplify it with similar tools. Of course, I am over generalizing here, but I hope I can give you an image. It's like learning to drive. What did you do? Did you get in a car and do it step-by-step, or did you spend years analyzing information to learn "the best way" or the best program? Did you go to school or read a book to learn how to drive? I hope this example will give you a solid image of what I mean by information overload or over-intellectualization. I myself am a really practical person and to be honest I prefer to try things and immerse myself in them to see if they work for me or not. As my late grandpa used to say, "The simplest things are always the best!"

-Add more indigo and purple into your life in the form of clothes or home accessories

-Mediate with blue. Staring at the stars, or a blue sky is great. Try to be outside as much as possible (I think this is what I say in each chapter of this book)

-Listen to classical music like Mozart or Beethoven

-Read spiritual books, or listen to guided meditations and hypnosis programs

-Add more 'brain foods' into your diet, foods that are rich in healthy omega-3 fatty acids like nuts, fish, avocados, or coconut oil

-Eat more blueberries and strawberries and use them for smoothies- these are great memory 'brain foods' as well

-Start a dream journal, it's fun! Especially when you start reading it and noticing patterns and that your dreams may be connected or appear as sequences and episodes. It's like watching a TV program that is operating in your subconscious mind

-Having problems? Looking for answers? Ask for patience, that's the first thing. It will fall into place. Keep asking the Universe and your subconscious mind. Take action to achieve what you want, but do it from the point of confidence. Again, don't overdo things and don't over-think them. Trust your inner self and the Universe. You may notice that the answers will manifest themselves in the most amazing circumstances and people you will attract to your life!

Incantations

Om

Yoga

-Mudra

Bend your index, ring, and pinky fingers downwards. Make the midpoints of each finger touch their counterpart on the other hand in this position. Let your middle fingers stick upright and connect the two of them. Let your thumbs meet and angle them downwards. Your thumbs and index fingers (and the ring and pinky fingers behind them) will form a heart shape, while your middle fingers will look like a tall pyramid. Position your hands in front of your chest and use this for meditation.

-Child's Pose

Kneel on the floor. Let your buttocks and thighs fall down until they're in contact with your lower legs and feet. Lean forward gently until your chest touches the front of your thighs. Draw your arms back so that your forearms lay on the floor, with palms facing the ceiling. Put your forehead to the floor and meditate for a few minutes.

-Variation

Kneel down and clasp your hands behind you. Tuck your chin towards your chest then bend at your waist until your forehead reaches the floor. Allow your arms to go up over your back and hold your position for up to three minutes. Inhale and raise your upper body, including your chin and head. Exhale and release your grip. Place your arms back to the sides of your body.

-Dolphin Plank

Get down on your hands and knees. Bend your arms so that your elbow rests upon the floor and press your palms together. Stretch your legs back and prop yourself up with the balls of your feet. Stay in this position for one to two minutes while visualizing your third eye chakra being stimulated by the pose.

Body Work

-Doing anything that puts you in a mild state of trance will work on the third eye chakra. For example, meditative exercises such as yoga, qi gong, or mindful walking. Activities that make use of an altered state of consciousness or deal with the spiritual realm will also do, such as meditation or dream working.

-I also recommend you massage your face and head with coconut oil. Press the third eye point and squeeze your eyebrows. Massage your temples and your forehead to eliminate tension that very often is a sign of worry, anxiety, and over-thinking (there we go again!). Embrace simplicity in your life. Less is better!

Energy Work

-Imagine yourself going into your own third eye chakra. Experience its energy – its brightness, color, movement, and strength. Are there any dense particles floating around? Is the color duller than what you had hoped it would be? The things you notice will tell you about the condition of the subtle energies in the chakra.

-You can cleanse and strengthen this chakra by utilizing the power of visualization. At the level you are at right now, the laws of creation are not as rigid as they are on the material world. That means you can create things out of your thought. Create tools that will manage the symptoms of an imbalanced third eye chakra – for example, torchlight for a dim chakra, a broom to sweep away the cobwebs that block your psychic sight, etc.

Aromatherapy

Use lavender, lemon, clary sage, vanilla, or jasmine essential oils

Mindset Change

-Psychic abilities are a natural part of being a human. The mind is capable of doing more things than what the majority of people know. It's because the mind is a function of the soul, which is a multidimensional entity that bypasses the limitations of space and time. There are some belief systems that prohibit the use of psychic abilities; you have the choice whether to adhere to them or not. Objectively though, people do have these abilities and they can learn how to hone them if they want to.

-There are many psychic development books and workshops out there; you will benefit a lot and expand your capabilities if you study them. If you have no experience with them yet, what you can do for now is to learn how to silence the chatter in your mind. Sharpen your senses and do your best to maintain attention to what's presently happening. Soon, perceptions will be streaming into your mind – this is what psychics use to gather information.

-You may have become skeptical of these psychic powers because it isn't encouraged in schools or society. To increase your confidence, research more about them. Find scientific studies – there is plenty of debunking material out there, but if you dig through the materials available to you, you will also find reliable research that proves the existence of psychic skills.

Natural Remedies

-Eating anything light and invigorating will resonate with the third eye chakra.

- Herbs & Spices

Use rosemary, lavender, poppy seed, or mugwort

Crystals

-Any indigo colored crystal (ex. Lapis Lazuli, amethyst, aquamarine)

Color therapy or being immersed in natural light is great for third eye chakra balancing

Sound Therapy

Meditating on the A note attunes the chakra to this frequency.

Interesting Information

This chakra is associated with the pineal gland, a small gland which is part of your endocrine system. It is responsible for producing melatonin that helps our bodies regulate our sleep-wake cycles. It's located between the two hemispheres of the brain and it controls our biorhythms, working closely with the hypothalamus gland to control our thirst, hunger, sexual desire, and aging (or anti-aging) processes.

Chapter 7 - Day 7 - The Seventh Chakra - The Spiritual Connection to Your Highest Potential and Fulfillment in All Areas of Life

The crown chakra, called Sahasrara in Sanscrit, is the seventh chakra, and it is considered as the highest of all the chakras on the spine. This represents the peak of spiritual growth. If this chakra is developed, the person will be able to meet the divinity that is called by many names – God, the Universe, the Source, the higher self, etc. It basically controls our thinking processes and also how we respond to the world around us.

Imbalances

Since the crown chakra symbolizes the ultimate goal of man, an imbalance of this chakra may lead to aimlessness and hollowness. Materialism is favored over spirituality, and this throws the person's progress back to the beginning. A simple example can be this: have a look at some wealthy people. Some of them, even though they have reached tremendous amounts of financial success, lack spirituality and purpose, and therefore feel unhappy. On the other hand, you also see people who are both wealthy and fulfilled- this is because aside from focusing on their wealth, they have also worked on other areas of their life and did not neglect their health and spirituality on the way.

It is also worth mentioning that a person may have an empty spirituality – for example, he or she will practice religious rituals without fully incorporating them to his or her being. How many times have you met people who claimed to believe in God, or claimed to be religious or spiritual, yet when you needed their help they were not there? There was no action, just empty words with no meaning at all. Of course, we are not here to judge. We are just saying and analyzing. As I said in the introduction, in my humble opinion, spirituality is about learning how to become a better version of yourself, contribution to society, and helping others. What is your definition of spirituality, by the way? You may let me and others know in the review section of this book.

Balancing Activities and Hobbies

-Read and listen to resources on self-acceptance

-Add sea salt to your bath or use it in your shower as a body peeling. This will also help you strengthen your aura, an electromagnetic field that surrounds your body

-Do not let your spirituality or spiritual practices make you feel better than those around you. Remember that everyone is on a different journey. Some people are still behind and some are way ahead of you. Everyone needs to follow their own pace. We are all equal. Nobody is better or worse. There is no judgment. Observe and accept

-Do not blame your circumstances for whatever obstacles you may be facing. Instead, see them as a learning experience to grow your spiritual and mental muscles

-Pray, and make it personal. You don't have to be a religious person to pray, and if you follow any religion, more mindful prayer will help you to explore it more. Keep it simple, you can set an intention for your day and ask the Universe for help. This is what I do every morning while journaling. I pick up one thing, one goal that I decide to focus on, and I ask the Divine force for strength, guidance, and perseverance. Try it and do it with an open mind. Mantras are also a form of prayer, and so is meditation and yoga. Some people prefer to go to church, it's all up to you. Follow your way and accept other people's ways.

-Try to disconnect from technology from time to time. You want to avoid distractions so that you can listen more closely to your inner self. Camping is great for that. Surround yourself with nature, ask questions, and wait patiently for answers. Patience is the key and my weak point I must admit, but I am learning to be more patient.

-As far as food is concerned, try to eat a more vegan diet, or choose lighter meals from time to time. Add more natural vegetable broths, juices, and soups into your diet and drink lots of clean water. I have a free guide with recipes (vegan-alkaline) that will help you. You can get it at:

www.bitly.com/AlkalineMarta

Affirmations

- I am safe as I follow my spiritual guidance
- My spirit helps me achieve my full potential
- I live a life of abundance, wisdom, and happiness
- I listen and I trust
- I take a meaningful and purposeful action
- I love learning new things
- Every day I become more aware of my actions
- Today I am stronger than I was yesterday
- I am blessed to be on the path of enlightenment

- I am connected to and supported by the Universe
- I am one with the Divine
- I am blissful
- I open myself to enlightenment
- My life has a meaning
- I am one with the Universe
- I accept the reality around me
- I am focused
- I feel directed and guided by the Light

Mantra

Om or Ah

Yoga

-Mudra

Place your hands near your stomach and clasp them together, fingers interlocking. Let your two ring fingers point upwards and connect with one another

-Thunderbolt Pose

Kneel with your bottom resting on your heels. Look ahead and rest your hands on your knees with your thumbs and index fingers touching. Stay still in this pose for 3 minutes

-Standing Backbend

Stand with your spine erect and your feet flat on the floor. Put your hands in front of your chest in a prayer position. Gradually raise your hands until they're in front of your face. Then, bend backward until you are facing the sky – maintain the position of your hands in front of your face.

Body Work

Meditative activities, or simply being in silence, can activate the crown chakra. Spiritual undertakings that make you feel enraptured by the divine also activate this ultra spiritual energy center.

Energy Work

Go to the top of your head and feel the energy present there. What feeling does it give you? Is it radiating pure light, or is it shadowy in some areas? Do you sense heaviness there? If you notice anything off with your crown chakra, ask the divine to help heal it. Do not doubt that this is possible. You don't have to make elaborate rituals for it, simply intend it with a sincere heart. After all, you are closest to the divine at this location on your body.

Like what you did in the previous chakras, you should explore the things you perceive in this chakra. You may find representations of spiritual hurdles in there. Examine it and gather more information by interacting with what you see – you may talk to characters, ponder on visions, manipulate the energies, and so on.

You can use tools or just envision a brilliant violet or white light leading to the crown chakra.

Aromatherapy

-Sandalwood, frankincense, lavender, or jasmine. I especially recommend head massages. Blend the essential oils with quality base oils (like coconut oil, sweet almond, avocado, or another type) and massage your scalp. You may listen to a guided meditation or meditative music that helps you feel connected with the here and now.

Mindset Change

-This chakra is where you are supposed to be complete so that you can transcend yourself and your limitations. First of all, have you neglected the lower chakras and jumped ahead to the crown? An imbalance in the lower chakras may lead to an imbalanced crown chakra, so you have to go back and take care of what you missed (remember Maslow's hierarchy?). Life is all about holistic development. It is not meant for you to neglect yourself in favor of achieving something that should be the natural result of a life in order.

-Simple example: all areas of life are important. I have previously mentioned an example of a person committed to pursuing wealth while forgetting about the importance of health or family. Well, there is also the other side of the spectrum. Some people get too obsessed about health and forget about the importance of other aspects of survival like taking care of their financial wellness, or keeping track of their expenses. I am not judging. I have been guilty of that as well. But really, unless you decide to live in a monastery or choose a self-sustainable life on top of a hill somewhere, you will need to take care of your lower chakras that are connected to the Earth and survival. Materialistic things are not always bad, though. In my humble opinion, achieving financial security can help you feel balanced and safe and then you have more time and freedom for wellness, personal development, and spiritual practice. So, to sum up, if you want your 7th chakra to work at its optimal level, you cannot neglect the other chakras.

It's all interconnected! Going to the extreme (wanting to be too spiritual in order to stand out and feel superior, or getting too obsessed about money) can lead to negativity and imbalances but... What if you can pursue both wealth and health? You deserve to have both. You deserve to have success and balance in all areas of your life, not just one. This is what I teach in all my books, programs, and also on my blog HolisticWellnessProject.com

This is what differentiates me from many health coaches who focus entirely on healthy recipes and similar activities related only to physical health. Don't get me wrong, they do a great job and their work is more than helpful in many people's lives and transformations. Again, I am not judging (I am repetitive, I know, but I want to make sure my message does not get distorted). However, my approach has always been truly holistic and also realistic. I believe that with the proper amount of work, effort, and commitment, you can increase your quality of life to have more health, greater relationships, more inner happiness, as well as fulfillment and financial security doing what you love. I think it's all possible. It all comes down working on your body, mind, and spirit. This is what you are doing right now and I applaud you for that! You can have vibrant health, the ideal lifestyle, love, and enough money to help you live the life you want. Just don't limit yourself, move forward, and be mindful about whatever it is that you are doing.

-Consider your conception of the Divine. You can achieve spiritual illumination even if you are an atheist as long as you have the drive to connect to something bigger than yourself. After all, God can take different forms, it doesn't have to be an actual God for it to be divine. It doesn't even have to be something that you understand. The divine simply *is*, and all you have to do to become illuminated by the divine is to reach out to it.

-Reflect on the divine – the more you reflect, the easier it will be for your mind to open up to it. Or, you can simply remain silent and let the light shine in. Whatever works for you is fine, regardless of your personal religious beliefs.

Questions to Ask Yourself:

Am I open to my own destiny?

Am I open to magic in my life?

Do I learn new things?

Are there any issues that I am fighting and trying to control right now?

Am I open to my own spirituality?

Am I scared to embrace my own spirituality?

Natural Remedies

Gotu Kola, Lotus, and Lavender

Crystals

Purple or white crystals (ex. amethyst, seraphinite, clear quartz)

Sound Therapy

Meditating on the B note attunes the chakra to this frequency.

Conclusion

Having balanced chakras is your ticket to living an amazing and fulfilled life. The meditations and exercises are fun and easy to do; the challenging part is to remain committed in making lifestyle changes so that your chakras remain healthy.

Here are some tips to help you stick to your commitment to helping yourself:

1. Make a list of your goals and your reminders to yourself. The mind is a very flexible thing, which is both good and bad at the same time. It's good because it can adapt and improve itself, but bad because it can make you abandon long-term goals in favor of what's easy and rewarding for the short term. On the other hand, a list is static. It doesn't transform itself because of subtle things like passing influences or moods. If you have this list, you will have something to go back to every time you find yourself drifting away.

2. Be perceptive. Feedback guides actions, and you will only get feedback if somebody else gives it to you or if you pay attention to what you're doing. It may not be possible for you to be mindful all the time, but at least set aside a few minutes every day to pay attention to yourself. It will be helpful if you have a diary so you can recall what happened during the day

and set plans for the coming day. Aside from evaluating your activities and experiences, practice sensing energy. This will connect your ordinary mind with your psychic mind. When you get used to functioning psychically, you will automatically sense if your chakras are out of alignment. Afterwards, you will be intuitively guided in what to do to bring back your balance.

3. Have a chakra remedy kit collection ready. Set aside perfumes, crystals, and activity tools that are connected with each chakra. This will prep you to focus on a particular chakra that seems imbalanced for you.

4. Write in a journal. A journal serves as a means to express yourself and record your experiences. It serves as your outlet and your record. It reflects your progress and makes you see what might still need some attention. It presents to you a clearer picture of your chakra states, and from that understanding, helps you create solutions to problems.

5. Always love yourself. Love is said to be the most powerful energy in the universe. Do not be harsh on yourself, none of us are perfect and we're here on earth to learn and improve the state of our soul. Congratulate yourself for challenges you have overcome, and encourage yourself during weak times. Don't be afraid to reach out for help – there are plenty of people out there who are glad to work on their crown chakras in the spirit

of service. Take this as an adventure that you will benefit from, no matter what happens.

Finally...what is the recipe for personal success?

It's simple. Instead of wasting your time trying to find more information or "the best way" to do something, focus on why you want t o do it. Having a strong WHY guides you in finding your HOW. Whenever you finish absorbing a new resource, whether it's a book, program, course, podcast, or an audiobook, pick up one thing from it. Just one thing that really resonated with you in that given moment. Commit to that thing. Then, you can move onto the next thing. Maybe next year you decide to re-read the book and your mind will pick up another 'one thing'. We always change, and so does our energy. Forget about looking for "the best stuff". You are the best! And just because you are the best, you always attract the best solutions. Be intuitive and listen to your body and mind. Stick to what works for you, but don't be afraid to leave your comfort zone every now and then and try new stuff. In my case, it's crystals. I used to think it was all magical hocus pocus, but now I am recognizing my pride and sarcasm. I am immersing myself in the world of crystals and learning more about it, and this is what I also share in this book. I am an aromatherapy type of lady, I was even dubbed an 'oil lady', heh, but…I need to regularly pick up one new thing so as to grow, learn, and stretch.

So, let me ask you, what was that one thing you have gotten from this read? Could you please share it in the review section of this book along your honest feedback about my work? It would be really, really appreciated. It's you I am writing for, and your opinion is of great importance to me. It will only take a few seconds for you to post a short review, even 1 sentence will suffice. But this one sentence you will write will surely put a smile on my face!

You can also contact me via e-mail:

info@holisticwellnessproject.com

If you happen to have any questions, suggestions, or doubts, I am here to help. I am also up for feedback. I am always looking for ways to improve myself and my work. Thanks in advance for helping me on my journey, it's really much appreciated.

For more inspiration and empowerment visit my blog:

www.HolisticWellnessProject.com

There is a free complimentary eBook: "Holistically Productive" waiting for. Download it today and enjoy your body and mind transformation like you deserve!

www.holisticwellnessproject.com/free-ebook/giveaway.html

With love, light, and respect,

I wish you holistic success in everything that you do,

Marta Tuchowska

MORE HOLISTIC WELLNESS BOOKS BY MARTA

To check out more of my books and articles (wellness, health, personal development, spirituality, spa, natural therapy, healthy recipes, alkaline diet, raw foods and much much more), please visit:

www.amazon.com/author/mtuchowska

www.holisticwellnessproject.com/personal-development-books

HEALING TIME!

If you are into healing, I especially recommend you grab this special, 3 in 1 Holistic healing BOX SET (3 for the price of 2). It will help you get where you want and need to be:

You can preview it at:

www.amazon.com/dp/B00ZO2QQK2

Finally, I would love to keep in touch with you for years to come!

Let's connect

www.facebook.com/HolisticWellnessProject

www.udemy.com/u/martatuchowska

www.pinterest.com/MartaWellness

www.plus.google.com/+MartaTuchowska

www.twitter.com/Marta_Wellness

www.linkedin.com/in/MartaTuchowska

www.goodreads.com/author/show/7520321.Marta_Tuchowska

One more thing…please, please help me by leaving a review for this book.

Visit Amazon at:

www.amazon.com/dp/B010HKU9Z8

click on "customers reviews" and then on "create your own" and let me know what you think. I will be very happy to hear from you!

Thanks in advance!

CPSIA information can be obtained
at www.ICGtesting.com
Printed in the USA
LVOW03s0049300517

536194LV00027B/696/P

9 781514 737019